The London Treasure Trail

This edition first published in 2012 by
Step Outside Guides.

ISBN 978-1-908921-00-0
Printed and bound in Great Britain by Berforts Group Ltd.

Acknowledgements

Our sincere thanks to Derrick Hudson, the creator of Baby Tembo, for allowing us to use his little elephant.

Thank you to all the people who have trialled the trail for us; Lizzy, Louis & Emma Froome; Guy, Claire, Ellie and Lara Hall; Katherine Taylor, Eleanor, Dylan and Lily Palmer and Phoebe Skinner.
Thanks also to Miranda and Duncan Brown, Joanne Ross and Teresa Solomon for their encouragement, guidance and expertise. Many other friends, and our families have helped and contributed in all sorts of ways, and for this we are very grateful.

A special thank you to Sam for bringing Baby Tembo to life.

Cover pictures
From top to bottom:
A Routemaster bus
The Old Curiosity Shop
The Albert Memorial

Every effort has been made to ensure that the information in this book is as accurate as possible at the time of going to press. However, details such as phone numbers and opening hours may change, and we suggest that you ring or check online in advance to avoid disappointment.
The authors and publishers can accept no responsibility for any loss, injury, or inconvenience sustained by any person as a result of information or advice in this guide.
Any view or opinions expressed in this book are solely those of the authors and do not necessarily represent those of the venues described.

The London
Treasure Trail

for Malcolm and Martyn

A Step Outside Guide

CONTENTS

Travel Tips

● Travelcards give unrestricted travel on buses, trains and Underground any time after 9.30am on weekdays, and all day at weekends.

● If you are travelling from outside the Travelcard area, ask at your station for the best way of including central London buses in your ticket (it may be cheapest to buy a bus ticket separately when you get to London).

● Tube maps are available free at every Underground station.

● The Transport for London website is www.tfl.gov.uk

INTRODUCTION

Hello! My name is Baby Tembo, and I live here in London. I'm from Africa, as you can see by my magnificent ears, and my name is African, too - Tembo is Swahili for Elephant. Mr Derrick Hudson created me in 2006 and he has kindly allowed me to be your guide on our London Treasure Trail.

Today I want to take you to all sorts of lovely places, including the sparkliest street in London and a house with a whole world of treasure inside it. I'm going to show you where I live, and we're going to finish up at a garden in the sky!

We're not going to rush — it's much nicer and more interesting if we take our time. We're going on two bus rides, too, and for the second, longer ride there's my special Bus Ride Guide to help you spot things as we go by.

Look at pages six and seven to check you have everything ready, and then we're all set for a terrific day out together!

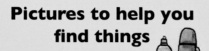

How to use your book

Pictures to help you find things

Good picnic spots

Accessibility information for buggies and wheelchairs

Free toilets

Top Treasure Alert!

You are about to see one of my special things or places!

Tick the jewel when you have seen it.

What to wear or bring with you

Comfortable shoes

Your picnic

Pencils and pens for *Rest your legs* pages

Your camera

Binoculars if you have some

Clothes and extras that suit the weather

IMPORTANT SAFETY INFORMATION

• Remember that London is very big and very busy; drivers can be fast and impatient.

• Only cross the road at traffic lights or pedestrian crossings.

• Make sure your group stays close together - no-one wants to get lost!

Road works

In a city there are often road works and building repairs going on. A building we've mentioned may be behind scaffolding, or a road closed. This is unpredictable, so it's best to just take it as part of London life, and enjoy any diversions. You may even discover something wonderful. Let us know at *www.stepoutsideguides.com*

Useful information and accessibility

Buses All buses can accommodate wheelchairs, except for the old Routemasters. The no.9 route also runs with modern buses.

Hatton garden
Many shops are open at weekends, but may be closed on Bank Holidays.
Check on
www.hatton-garden.net

Kensington Roof Garden
Entrance at 99 Derry Street W8
Tel 020 7937799**4**
www.roofgardens.virgin.com
Lift access.
Important:
May close for private functions. Check by phoning up to one week ahead.

Sir John Soane's House
13 Lincoln's Inn Fields
London
WC2A 3BP
Tel 020 7405 2107
www.soane.org

Open Tuesday – Saturday
10.00 am – 5.00pm
(Closed Sunday, Monday.)

St Clement Danes Church
'Oranges and Lemons' plays on the bells daily at 9.00am, 12.00 noon, 3.00pm, 6.00pm, 9.00pm.

Ring ahead of your visit to enable staff to help you with access to the museum.

READY, STEADY, GO...

Starting Point:
Chancery Lane Underground Station **Central line**
Finishing Point:
Kensington High Street Station **Circle** & **District** Lines
Walking distance: about 5km, 3 miles.
Time: About five hours at a leisurely pace, with breaks.

We're going to leave Chancery Lane station by exit 2, 'to Holborn Circus'.

Now set off along High Holborn past the splendid, HUGE red brick Prudential Insurance building on our left. What decorations can you spot above the windows?

High Holborn is a funny road; just look at the middle of it! There are masses of bikes and motor bikes parked there, with statues in amongst them, and some very grand toilets (which always seem to be closed – how silly!)

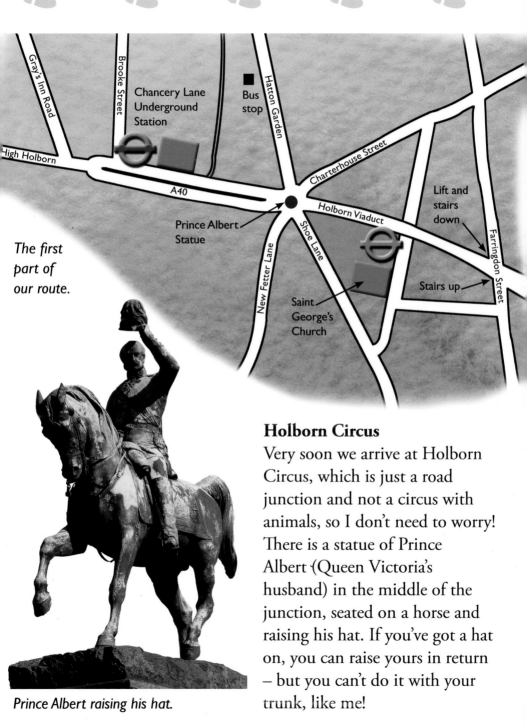

Gray's Inn Road

Brooke Street

Chancery Lane
Underground
Station

Hatton Garden

Bus
stop

High Holborn

A40

Charterhouse Street

Holborn Viaduct

Lift and
stairs
down

Farringdon Street

Prince Albert
Statue

Shoe Lane

*The first
part of
our route.*

New Fetter Lane

Saint
George's
Church

Stairs up

Prince Albert raising his hat.

Holborn Circus

Very soon we arrive at Holborn Circus, which is just a road junction and not a circus with animals, so I don't need to worry! There is a statue of Prince Albert (Queen Victoria's husband) in the middle of the junction, seated on a horse and raising his hat. If you've got a hat on, you can raise yours in return – but you can't do it with your trunk, like me!

London Borough of Camden
HATTON GARDEN
E.C.1

The very first road on our left at Holborn Circus is Hatton Garden, and this is our first treasure–real treasure shops!

They aren't exactly hidden away, but although they are right in the middle of London, this is not a busy street. It doesn't look very spectacular at first, but wait until you look in the windows. We're going to walk up the left hand side of Hatton Garden as far as the junction with

Greville Street. We'll find my first Top Treasure on the way. Outside the shop Holts, at number 98, is a great big **geode,** or crystal cave. The purple crystals are amethyst, and this is how they naturally 'grow'.

Aren't they beautiful? I like this better than any of the gemstones in the windows, even though it isn't worth nearly as much money.

When we get to the junction with Greville Street, it's time to cross the road and walk back to the Prince-Albert-and-his-Hat statue, passing more treasure shops as we go.

INFORMATION
Many shops stay open at the weekend, but check on Bank Holidays as the whole street may be closed.

This road is named after Sir Christopher Hatton. Queen Elizabeth I gave him the land in 1576.

Who can spot the most expensive piece of jewellery? How much does it cost?

Who has spotted the biggest jewel?

There are zillions of pounds worth of jewels in Hatton Garden. They must be VERY closely guarded. But there aren't lots of policemen or security people around.
I wonder how they keep all this treasure safe!
What do you think?

What colour gemstone do you like the best? My favourite is peridot.

Peridot is a gentle green colour. It can be found all over the world.

This area has been the centre of London's jewellery trade since medieval times.

HOLBORN VIADUCT EC1

Back at Holborn Circus, we need to cross the next street round on the left, Charterhouse Street, and walk a little way along Holborn Viaduct.

Just before the second set of dark red railings, there is an elegant white building. We're going through its arch and down the stairs or lift to the street below. What a huge and fabulous picture on the stairwell wall!

Can you see what it is all about? It shows the viaduct being built. I bet there were some big horsey traffic jams while that was happening!

Holborn Circus

On the left of the picture, look out for the square church tower. This is Saint Andrew's church at Holborn Circus. We are going to see the real one in a few minutes.

This is the picture, it shows the viaduct being built in the1860s

> **Holborn Viaduct**
> I love this bridge-road – or is it a road-bridge? It was built in the 1860s. The Victorians really built with style – it must have cost a fortune! Just look at the decorations: helmets-with-wings???

The Viaduct

Before that, we're going to walk right under the viaduct. So, out onto Farringdon Street we go, and turn right. Look up at the struts holding up the viaduct.

See if you can find this dragon.

you - how many are there?
Alternatively, you can return to the lift, then cross the road at the top.

They are jolly dirty, but the dragons and the other decorations are fantastic! This must have looked wonderful when it was clean and new; it makes me want to wash it!

Time for the first bus ride!

At the top of the stairs, we turn left and walk about 125 paces (about 150 baby elephant steps). Our bus stop is labelled 'L'. It's right by St Andrew's church, which we saw in the big picture.

There is a churchyard right beside it, where we can have a rest if you need one.

When we get to the other side of the viaduct, we will find another set of steps which take us back to the top. Look out for four red dragons, and lots of faces watching

St Andrew's Church today

GT TURNSTILE
Leading to
LINCOLN'S INN FIELDS
◄———————◄◄

We can jump on any of the buses that come along. The third stop, Brownlow Street, is ours. Listen out for the announcement. It's right outside a very posh cake shop, called 'Paul'. It's such a shame I don't eat cakes!

Great Turnstile What a brilliant name for a street! Hundreds of years ago, when cattle grazed in Lincoln's Inn Field, there was a turnstile here to stop them wandering out into busy High Holborn.

The Great Turnstile probably looked rather like this.

Once we're off the bus we walk on, past the pub called 'Penderel's Oak', and then turn left straight away, down Great Turnstile. At the end of this little street, we find ourselves in Lincoln's Inn Fields, and near our next treasure.

INFORMATION
Sir John Soane's Museum is open from Tuesday to Saturday, and from 10.00am to 5.00pm It is closed on Sundays and Mondays.
www.soane.org

SIR JOHN SOANE'S HOUSE

We need to turn right and walk about half way along, to the Sir John Soane's Museum at number 13.

We have to be VERY careful in the house because there are lots of wonderful but fragile things. I must remember not to swing my trunk.

Although it is called a museum, the house is almost exactly as it was when Sir John lived in it about 200 years ago. I am really excited about showing you inside here! We may have to queue for a little while to get in, but it is worth the wait.

Sir John Soane
lived from 1753 to 1837, and he was an important architect; he designed the Bank of England, and there aren't many buildings more important than that! All his life he collected bits of ancient buildings, paintings, sculptures, drawings and lots of other stuff besides - as you will see!

First we walk through the elegant dining room and library.

Have a look at the astronomical clock near the window; can you see the model of the planets moving around the sun at the top of the clock? How clever is that! Teasel heads on the chairs remind us not to sit on this old and fragile furniture. It's definitely not made for elephants - even baby ones!

As we move into the next room, the magic really begins. Sir John's house is crammed with wonderful things: statues and carvings, models and paintings, urns, bits of ancient buildings, stained glass windows and even a hieroglyph-smothered Egyptian Sarcophagus (coffin). It all looks rather like a film set! What kind of film do you think might be made here? Write a title in the space.

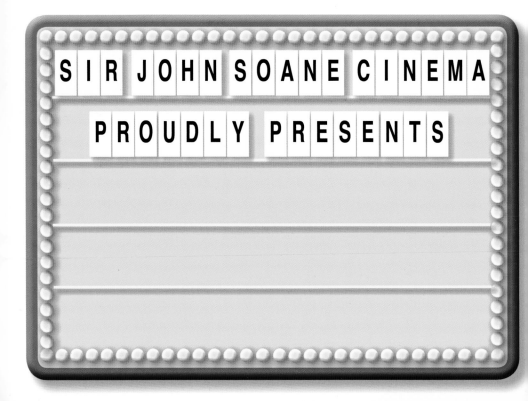

SIR JOHN SOANE CINEMA

PROUDLY PRESENTS

Top Treasure!

What is your John Soane Top Treasure? Write it here!

Name	Your Top Treasure
Baby Tembo	The Picture Room

The Picture room is my next Top Treasure. Although it is small, it contains over 100 large pictures. How can this be? If we are lucky, there will be someone from the museum here to show us how all the walls swing out to reveal other pictures, hidden behind. And these aren't just any pictures - some of them are very famous and important. One wall has three layers of pictures hidden away! So this is my hidden treasure, hidden in a hidden treasure!

Look up!
Don't forget to look up - some of the ceilings are richly decorated, while others are made of coloured glass, which casts a gentle light on everything.

LINCOLN'S INN FIELDS WC2
CITY OF WESTMINSTER

Phew! That was fantastic, but now, it's definitely time for a break, and maybe a picnic too. My lunch is six bunches of bananas!

Let's leave Sir John's house, cross the road and go into the square opposite by the nearest gate.

If we turn right, we'll see a seat with a bronze sculpture of a lady and children all along the top of it. This is dedicated to a lady called Margaret Macdonald "who spent her life helping others". What a lovely way to be remembered! Even now, after her death, she is helping people to rest. This is a nice spot for lunch, but if it's full there are plenty of other places we can sit.

Rest-your-legs page

Here's a jewel word search. How many words can you find?

AMETHYST, DIAMOND, EMERALD, GARNET, GOLD, NECKLACE, PERIDOT, PLATINUM, RING, RUBY, SAPPHIRE, SILVER, TEMBO, TOPAZ

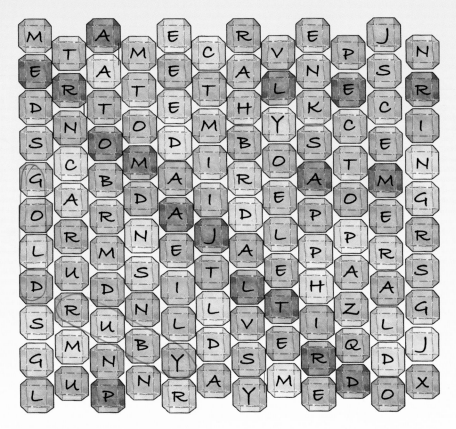

Solution to puzzle p.30

What would you like to give me
for lunch? Draw it in my trunk!

Right, are you rested and revived? It's time for us to get up and on to find some more treasure, right here in the square.

Where we came into the square is a Catalpa tree. It has hundreds of HUGE beans hanging down. Can you see them?

A plane tree trunk - it looks like an elephant's trunk!

Catalpa tree with beans

It's a jungle! Home at last. It's not very big, but I love it here; it is so lush and overgrown, it feels as though there should be wild animals here too!

From here, we're going to walk to the centre of the square, where there is a bandstand.

Shall we pretend to be a band? I could play the trumpet! Turn left, and we'll pass under a gigantic old London plane tree.

Can you see just how far the branches stretch out? Near the end of the path is a little turning to the right, and here is my next Top Treasure.

Which animal would you like to meet?

Which would you like *NOT* to meet?

CLARE MARKET WC2
CITY OF WESTMINSTER

Now I'm getting really excited, because we're getting close to my Toppiest Top Treasure. It is – ahem – the statue of me! I've drawn a little map to show you how to find me.

When we leave the Square, we go down Portsmouth Street. Just where Portsmouth Street bends is 'The Old Curiosity Shop', made famous by Charles Dickens' book of the same name. Turn right into Portugal Street, and take the second turning on the left, which is Clare Market.
By the slope up to the building on the right – **THERE I AM**!
Can you see me?

We are now right in the middle of the London School of Economics. If it's term time, I can watch the students milling about. They have come from all over the world to study here.

MY MAP TO ME!

It's me! The real Baby Tembo!

BABY TEMBO

Are you going to take a photo of me? Shall we have a photo taken together? Lovely! Just near me, on the other side of the path is my friend Pedro Penguin. Go on – give him a hug!

Well, wave goodbye and on we go, turning right at the end of Clare Market, into Houghton Street, and from there in to the big, curving road ahead, Aldwych.

We're in for a treat now – a bus ride right through the middle of London, to Kensington and to our last, very exciting treasure. But first we have to get to the bus stop, which is a bit of a palaver; here we go!

Turn left into Aldwych and walk to the end, where we cross Strand, and pass the statue of William Gladstone on our left. Now, cross the other part of Strand, then we turn right and cross Arundel Street, and walk to the number 9 bus stop, labelled 'R'. It is opposite another church in the middle of the road, called 'St Mary le Strand'.

Here is a map to help you find the bus stop

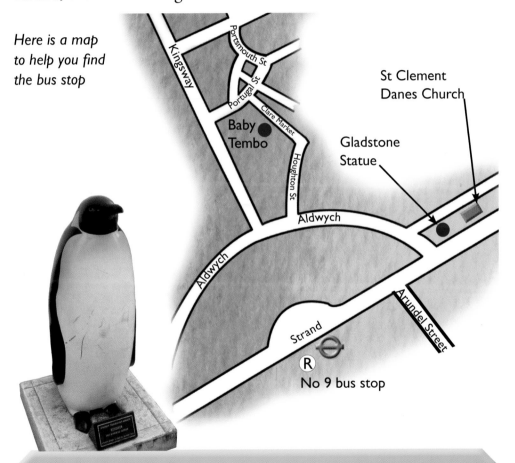

Oranges and Lemons

Behind Gladstone's statue is a church in the middle of the road. It is St Clement Danes, and if you happen to be here at 9.00am, 12.00 noon, 3.00pm or 6.00pm, you can hear the bells playing 'Oranges and Lemons'.

A SPECIAL BUS RIDE

The number 9 bus ride is definitely a Top Treasure, and here's why! Firstly, we'll see lots of London's famous sights as we travel along.

Secondly, we are getting on the bus right at the beginning of the route, so with luck you'll be able to bag the seats right at the front upstairs for the most brilliant view possible. And thirdly, some of the buses that run route number 9 are the old 'Routemaster' buses. Sadly, they don't start until further along the route, but we'll see quite a few passing us. Who can spot one first?

This lovely ride will last for about half an hour, and I've written a guide for you, to help you to

 spot some of the special London sights we'll be passing. Here we go!

Routemaster Buses

From about 1960 until 2003, Routemaster buses were used all over London. They were gradually exchanged for new, accessible and modern buses, but everyone missed the lovely old buses so much that they were brought back on two routes through the middle of London, including our number 9. Let's hope they keep running forever!

Baby Tembo's Bus Ride Guide

Here are some of the highlights of our bus trip through the middle of London – tick them off as we pass.

Trafalgar Square with Nelson's Column reaching to the sky.

Duke of York Column on our left. The Grand Old Duke of York; When he was up he was up - and there he is! But he's still not as high up as Nelson!

Piccadilly Circus with the statue of Eros and LOADS of bright, electric advertisements.

Piccadilly a wide, famous road. On the left we pass the beautifully decorated shop windows of *Fortnum and Mason*, then the *Ritz Hotel* and *Green Park*. On the right are the *Royal Academy of Arts* for people who like quiet, serious things, and near the other end is the *Hard Rock Café* for people who like noise and fun.

Hyde Park Corner where *Green Park* and *Hyde Park* meet. There is a huge archway on the roundabout – can you see it? It is called the *Wellington Arch*, and on the top there is a huge sculpture of the *Angel of Peace* driving a chariot with four horses. This carriage is called a *Quadriga*: bet you didn't know that! *What might a chariot drawn by four elephants be called?* ....
Our number 9 bus runs along the edge of Hyde Park to Knightsbridge.

The Albert Memorial on the right – a huge, richly decorated monument for Queen Victoria's beloved husband (this is the same man who was raising his hat to us at Holborn Circus).

The Royal Albert Hall opposite the memorial, on our left. Can you see the frieze of pictures around the top of this nearly-circular hall?

Queen's Gate just past the Albert Memorial; beautiful gates with statues of deer and their fawns at each end.

Kensington Palace peeping through the trees in the park.

KENSINGTON ROOF GARDEN

We're nearly at our last treasure now. When you hear the bus announcer say 'Kensington Palace', then you know that our stop, 'High Street Kensington Station', is next. So give your legs a shake, pick up your bags, and off we go.

We need to walk past the station, past Marks and Spencer, and then turn right down Derry Street. Number 99 is on the right and we're going inside. It looks a bit scary, but the people there are very nice and friendly. Ask to see the garden.

Everyone will have to sign the

book, and then a posh lift will whisk us up to the roof. At the top jump out, go to the little water-

fall and turn right – and WOW!

A beautiful garden in the sky! There are trees and waterfalls, bridges and statues, beautiful plants and flowers and even ducks and flamingos! The roofs of other buildings and a big church spire peek in at the edges. There are windows to look out over London, and plenty of seats to sit and rest.

It's easy to forget that we are six floors up! Let's take our time, and enjoy this AMAZING hidden treasure.

Rest-your-legs page

Draw people in the windows of the bus and put an advertisement on the banner on the side.

Have a competition to see who can stand on one leg for the longest time.

How many words can you make out of BABY TEMBO? There is extra space on page 31.

....

....

....

My Top Treasure here? The flamingos, of course!

Here's a picture of me trying to stand like a flamingo; it's harder than it looks!

This is the largest roof garden in Europe! In the 1930s, this building was a department store called Derry and Toms.

The chairman, Trevor Bowen had the idea for a 'garden in the sky', and there is a plaque to honour him on one of the garden walls.
See if you can find it.

Today the gardens are 'Grade Two Listed'. This means that they mustn't be spoiled or destroyed. Sir Richard Branson owns them now, and he kindly allows us to come and see this beautiful place for free!

The Roof Garden has three themed areas:
1) A Spanish Garden with fountains, covered walkways, pink walls and bright, bright flowers.

2) A Tudor-style garden with archways and secret corners. In summer it is filled with roses and lavender, and smells beautiful!

3) An English woodland garden, with over a 100 trees! There are 30 different types of tree, and some of them have been here for over 60 years. They seem happy, even though they only have one metre of soil to grow in. There is also a pretty stream (a stream! On a roof! My goodness!) and a pond that is home to pintail ducks and four flamingos. Sometimes, when no-one is looking, I suck up water with my trunk and give the birds a lovely shower!

When it's time to go, we'll go back to the lift, down to the ground floor, sign out in the book, back past Marks and Spencer to High Street Kensington station, and this is where I have to leave you.

I hope you've enjoyed our day together; I certainly have! I hope you'll come and visit me again one day.

Byeeeeee!

JUST IN CASE...

Occasionally, the Roof Garden is closed for a private function. If it is, then I've got an alternative plan for you.

Stay on the bus to the other end of Kensington High Street. Get off at the 'Kensington High Street, Earls Court' stop, and visit Holland Park instead. The gates are next to the Commonwealth Institute, which will become the Design Museum.

At first it looks like a normal park, but cross the field to the building at the back and you will find:

- A big adventure playground
- Peacocks
- Woodland walks
- A nature play area
- A sundial with HUGE tortoises
- Formal gardens
- A Japanese garden

And there's lots of room for elephants - and yo'

Here is the solution to the word search on page 19, did you find all the words?

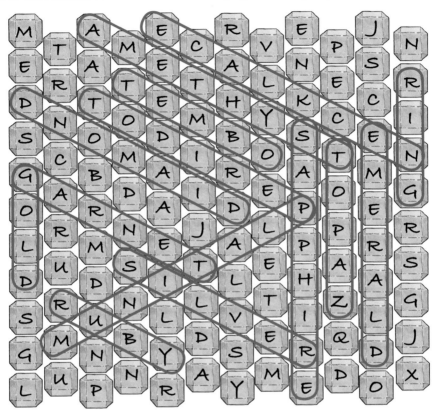

We hope you have enjoyed your day in London with
Step Outside Guides.
If you'd like to let us know what you got up to, or what
extra treasures you found, you can leave a message at
feedback@stepoutsideguides.com
If you'd like pictures of your day to be in our online gallery,
send them to
gallery@stepoutsideguides.com

Notes

Notes